BOTANICAL SANCTUARIES

Pennsylvania Ecoregions

- Eastern Great Lakes Lowlands
- Middle Atlantic Coastal Plain
- North Central Appalachians
- Western Allegheny Plateau
- Central Appalachians
- Erie Drift Plain
- Blue Ridge
- Northeastern Highlands
- Northern Piedmont
- Ridge and Valley

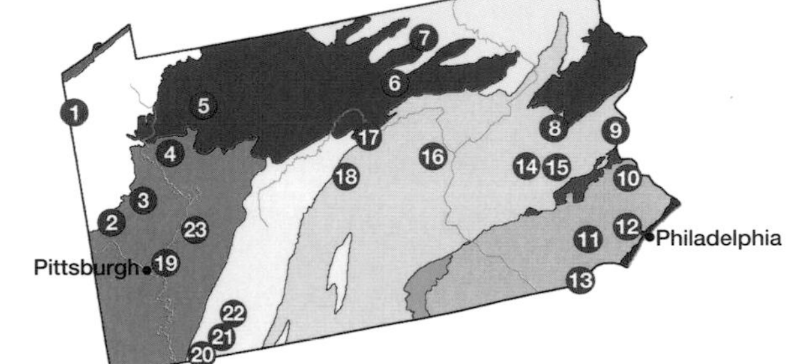

Pittsburgh
Philadelphia

1. Blackjack Swamp/ Pymatuning State Park
2. Slippery Rock Creek Gorge/ McConnell's Mill State Park
3. Moraine State Park
4. Cook Forest State Park
5. Allegheny National Forest
6. Little Pine State Park
7. Mt. Pisgah State Park
8. Hickory Run State Park
9. Delaware Water Gap National Recreation Area
10. Bowman's Hill Wildflower Preserve
11. French Creek State Park
12. Jenkins Arboretum
13. Longwood Gardens
14. Locust Lake State Park
15. Tuscarora State Park
16. Rapid Run Natural Area/ R.B. Winter State Park
17. Kettle Creek State Park
18. Black Moshannon State Park
19. Phipps Conservatory & Botanical Gardens
20. Forbes State Forest
21. Ferncliff Peninsula/ Ohiopyle State Park
22. Laurel Hill State Park
23. Pittsburgh Botanic Garden

Measurements denote the height of plants unless otherwise indicated. Illustrations are not to scale.

N.B. – Many edible wild plants have poisonous mimics. Never eat a wild plant or fruit unless you are absolutely sure it is safe to do so. The publisher makes no representation or warranties with respect to the accuracy, completeness, correctness or usefulness of this information and specifically disclaims any implied warranties of fitness for a particular purpose. The advice, strategies and/or techniques contained herein may not be suitable for all individuals. The publisher shall not be responsible for any physical harm (up to and including death), loss of profit or other commercial damage. The publisher assumes no liability brought or instituted by individuals or organizations arising out of or relating in any way to the application and/or use of the information, advice and strategies contained herein.

Waterford Press publishes reference guides that introduce readers to nature observation, outdoor recreation and survival skills. Product information is featured on the website: www.waterfordpress.com.

A POCKET NATURALIST® GUIDE

PENNSYLVANIA TREES & WILDFLOWERS

A Folding Pocket Guide to Familiar Plants

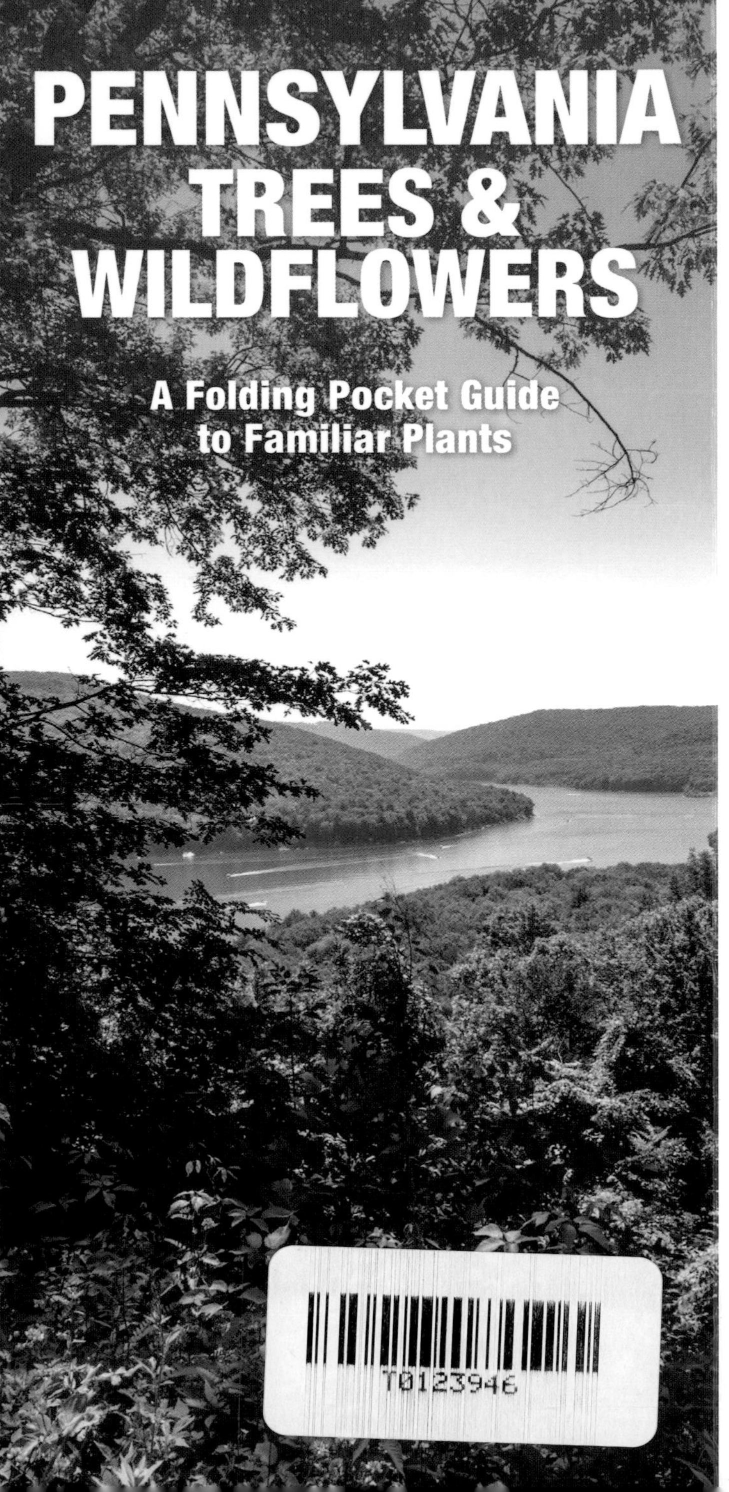

PENNSYLVANIA TREES & WILDFLOWERS – A Folding Pocket Guide to Familiar Plants

WATERFORD PRESS

Pitch Pine
Pinus rigida To 60 ft. (18 m)
Long needles grow in bundles of 3. Cone scales have stiff, curved spines. Bark is rich with resin (pitch).

Eastern White Pine
Pinus strobus To 100 ft. (30 m)
Needles grow in bundles of 5. Cone is up to 8 in. (20 cm) long.

Eastern Hemlock
Tsuga canadensis To 70 ft. (21 m)
Flat needles grow from 2 sides of twigs, parallel to the ground. Tip of tree usually droops. **Pennsylvania's state tree.**

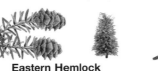

Eastern Redcedar
Juniperus virginiana To 60 ft. (18 m)
Four-sided branchlets are covered with overlapping, scale-like leaves. Fruit is a blue berry.

Yellow Poplar (Tuliptree)
Liriodendron tulipifera To 120 ft. (36.5 m)
Note unusual leaf shape. Showy flowers are succeeded by cone-like aggregates of papery, winged seeds.

Black Willow
Salix nigra To 100 ft. (30 m)
Tree or shrub, often leaning. Slender leaves are shiny green on the upper surface. Flowers bloom in long, fuzzy clusters.

Red Maple
Acer rubrum To 90 ft. (27 m)
Leaves have 3-5 lobes and turn scarlet in autumn. Flowers are succeeded by red, winged seed pairs.

Silver Maple
Acer saccharinum To 80 ft. (24 m)
Note short trunk and spreading crown. Five-lobed leaves are silvery beneath.

Sugar Maple
Acer saccharum To 100 ft. (30 m)
Leaves have five coarsely-toothed lobes. Fruit is a winged seed pair. Tree sap is the source of maple syrup.

Black Birch
Betula lenta To 80 ft. (24 m)
Leaves are saw-toothed. Twigs smell like wintergreen. Dark bark is brown to blackish.

American Beech
Fagus grandifolia To 80 ft. (24 m)
Flowers bloom in rounded clusters in spring and are succeeded by 3-sided nuts.

Cucumber Magnolia
Magnolia acuminata To 80 ft. (24 m)
Pointed leaves are up to 10 in. (25 cm) long. Named for its cone-like fruit.

Flowering Dogwood
Cornus florida To 30 ft. (9 m)
Tiny yellow flowers bloom in crowded clusters surrounded by 4 white petal-like structures.

White Oak
Quercus alba To 100 ft. (30 m)
Leaves have 5-9 rounded lobes. Acorn has a shallow, scaly cup.

Pin Oak
Quercus palustris To 90 ft. (27 m)
Leaves have 5-7 deep lobes. Thin twigs have pin-like spurs. Acorns are rounded.

Scarlet Oak
Quercus coccinea To 80 ft. (24 m)
Leaves have 5-9 spreading lobes and are up to 7 in. (18 cm) long. Leaves turn scarlet in fall.

Northern Red Oak
Quercus rubra To 90 ft. (27 m)
Large tree has a rounded crown. Leaves have 7-11 spiny lobes.

Black Oak
Quercus velutina To 80 ft. (24 m)
Leaves have 5-7 spiny lobes. Acorns have a ragged-edged cup.

Hawthorn
Crataegus spp. To 40 ft. (12 m)
Tree has rounded crown of spiny branches. Apple-like fruits appear in summer.

Boxelder
Acer negundo To 60 ft. (18 m)
Leaves have 3-7 leaflets. Seeds are encased in paired papery keys.

Green Ash
Fraxinus pennsylvanica To 60 ft. (18 m)
Leaves have 7-9 leaflets. Flowers are succeeded by single-winged fruits.

Black Walnut
Juglans nigra To 90 ft. (27 m)
Leaves have 9-23 leaflets. Greenish fruits have a black nut inside.

Horse Chestnut
Aesculus hippocastanum To 70 ft. (21 m)
Small flowers are succeeded by spiny green balls. Seeds are poisonous. Introduced ornamental.

Eastern Hophornbeam
Ostrya virginiana To 50 ft. (15 m)
Bark has a shreddy appearance. Hop-like fruits are hanging, cone-like clusters.

Honey Locust
Gleditsia triacanthos To 80 ft. (24 m)
Leaves have 7-15 pairs of leaflets. Twisted fruits are up to 16 in. (40 cm) long.

American Hornbeam
Carpinus caroliniana To 30 ft. (9 m)
Also called blue beech, it has blue-gray bark and a "muscular" trunk. Distinctive fruits have seeds contained in 3-sided bracts.

Red Mulberry
Morus rubra To 60 ft. (18 m)
Leaves are 3-lobed, oval or mitten-shaped. Elongate fruit is edible.

American Sycamore
Platanus occidentalis To 100 ft. (30 m)
Leaves have 3-5 shallow lobes. Rounded fruits are bristly.

Tree of Heaven
Ailanthus altissima To 80 ft. (24 m)
Introduced species is a widely-planted ornamental. Dense clusters of yellowish flowers are succeeded by papery keys.

Eastern Cottonwood
Populus deltoides To 100 ft. (30 m)
Leaves are up to 7 in. (18 cm) long. Flowers are succeeded by capsules containing seeds with cottony "tails."

Trembling Aspen
Populus tremuloides To 70 ft. (21 m)
Long-stemmed leaves rustle in the slightest breeze. The most widely distributed tree in North America.

Shagbark Hickory
Carya ovata To 100 ft. (30 m)
Bark curls away from the trunk, giving it a shaggy appearance. Leaves have 5 leaflets.

Ohio Buckeye
Aesculus glabra To 70 ft. (21 m)
Yellowish flowers bloom in erect clusters in spring. Named for its seeds that have a light "eye" spot.

Black Cherry
Prunus serotina To 80 ft. (24 m)
Aromatic bark and leaves smell cherry-like. Dark berries have an oval stone inside.

Bitternut Hickory
Carya cordiformis To 80 ft. (24 m)
Leaves have 7-11 leaflets. Bitter fruits are unpalatable to most wildlife.

American Basswood
Tilia americana To 100 ft. (30 m)
Flowers and nutlets hang from narrow leafy bracts.

Eastern Redbud
Cercis canadensis To 40 ft. (12 m)
Showy magenta, pea-shaped flowers are succeeded by oblong seed pods.

Black Locust
Robinia pseudoacacia To 80 ft. (24 m)
Leaves have 7-19 leaflets. Black seed pods are up to 4 in. (10 cm) long.

Sassafras
Sassafras albidum To 60 ft. (18 m)
Aromatic tree or shrub has leaves that are mitten-shaped or 3-lobed. Fruits are dark berries.

Common Chokecherry
Prunus virginiana To 20 ft. (6 m)
Cylindrical clusters of spring flowers are succeeded by dark, red-purple berries.

Witch Hazel
Hamamelis virginiana To 30 ft. (9 m)
Shrub or small tree. Tiny yellow flowers bloom along leafless twigs in the fall. Woody fruits eject their seeds when ripe.

Mountain Winterberry
Ilex montana To 30 ft. (9 m)
Spreading shrub or small tree. Bright red berries persist into winter. A holly relative.

Mountain Laurel
Kalmia latifolia To 20 ft. (6 m)
Evergreen shrub or small tree. Leaves are leathery. **State flower of Pennsylvania.**

Buttonbush
Cephalanthus occidentalis To 10 ft. (3 m)
"Pincushion" flowers have protruding stamens.

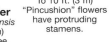

Serviceberry
Amelanchier spp.
To 15 ft. (4.5 m)
White, 5-petalled flowers bloom June-July and are succeeded by purplish, sweet fruits.

American Elder
Sambucus canadensis To 16 ft. (4.8 cm)
Shrub or small tree. Saw-toothed leaves have 3-7 leaflets. Flowers are succeeded by dark berries.

Arrowwood
Viburnum dentatum To 10 ft. (3 m)
Dense shrub has flattened clusters of creamy flowers that are succeeded by blue-black berries.

Smooth Sumac
Rhus glabra To 20 ft. (6 m)
Clusters of white flowers are succeeded by "hairy" red fruits. Bark is gray and smooth.

WHITE & GREENISH FLOWERS

Shooting Star
Dodecatheon spp.
To 20 in. (50 cm)
Flower petals are white, rose or lilac.

Dutchman's Breeches
Dicentra cucullaria
To 12 in. (30 cm)
Spurred flowers resemble trousers.

Indian Pipe
Monotropa uniflora
To 10 in. (25 cm)
Waxy white plant is parasitic on other plants in shady woods.

Fly Poison
Amianthium muscitoxicum
To 4 ft. (1.2 m)

Pearly Everlasting
Anaphalis margaritacea
To 3 ft. (90 cm)
Creamy flowers bloom in large terminal clusters.

White Snakeroot
Eupatorium rugosum
To 3 ft. (90 cm)

Queen Anne's Lace
Daucus carota
To 4 ft. (1.2 m)
Flower clusters become cup-shaped as they age.

Oxeye Daisy
Leucanthemum vulgare
To 3 ft. (90 cm)
Showy flowers bloom along roadsides in summer.

Jack-in-the-Pulpit
Arisaema triphyllum
To 3 ft. (90 cm)
Club-like stem is surrounded by a curving, green to purplish hood.

Cow Parsnip
Heracleum lanatum
To 9 ft. (2.7 m)
Grows in moist soils. Creamy white flowers bloom in dense, flattened clusters.

Grass of Parnassus
Parnassia glauca
To 20 in. (50 cm)

Philadelphia Fleabane
Erigeron philadelphicus
To 3 ft. (90 cm)

Fragrant Water Lily
Nymphaea odorata
Flower to 6 in. (15 cm) wide.

WHITE & GREENISH FLOWERS

Mayapple
Podophyllum peltatum
To 18 in. (45 cm)
Cup-shaped flowers bloom between 2 leaves. Fruits are yellow.

Bloodroot
Sanguinaria canadensis
To 10 in. (25 cm)
Blooms in early spring.

Horsenettle
Solanum carolinense
To 3 ft. (90 cm)
Note broad-toothed leaves and spiny stems. Flowers are white to pink.

Large-flowered Trillium
Trillium grandiflorum
To 18 in. (45 cm)
3 white petals turn pinkish with age.

Solomon's Zigzag
Maianthemum racemosum
To 3 ft. (90 cm)
Tiny flowers bloom in a dense terminal cluster and are succeeded by red berries. Note kinked stem.

Rue Anemone
Anemonella thalictroides
To 10 in. (25 cm)

YELLOW & ORANGE FLOWERS

Butterfly Weed
Asclepias tuberosa
To 3 ft. (90 cm)
Orange flowers are star-shaped.

Trout Lily
Erythronium americanum
To 10 in. (25 cm)
Common in meadows and rich woodlands.

Tickseed
Coreopsis lanceolata
To 2 ft. (60 cm)
Note lance-shaped leaves and notched flower rays.

Sneezeweed
Helenium amarum
To 20 in. (50 cm)
Yellow flowers have a dome-like central disk.

Jewelweed
Impatiens capensis
To 5 ft. (1.5 m)
Spotted, orange-yellow flowers are horn-shaped.

Common St. John's Wort
Hypericum perforatum
To 30 in. (75 cm)
Widespread weed is found in waste areas.

YELLOW & ORANGE FLOWERS

Goldenrod
Solidago spp.
To 5 ft. (1.5 m)
Flowers bloom in arched clusters.

Hoary Puccoon
Lithospermum canescens
To 18 in. (45 cm)

Downy Yellow Violet
Viola pubescens
To 16 in. (40 cm)

Butter-and-eggs
Linaria vulgaris
To 3 ft. (90 cm)
Spurred flowers have a patch of orange in the throat.

Common Evening Primrose
Oenothera biennis
To 5 ft. (1.5 m)
Lemon-scented, 4-petalled flowers bloom in the evening.

Devil's Tongue
Opuntia humifusa
To 12 in. (30 cm)
Clumps to 3 ft. (90 cm) wide.

Shrubby Cinquefoil
Potentilla simplex
Stems to 3 ft. (90 cm)
Sprawling roadside plant has leaves with 5 leaflets.

Buttercup
Ranunculus spp.
To 3 ft. (90 cm)
Flower petals are waxy to the touch.

Black-eyed Susan
Rudbeckia hirta
To 3 ft. (90 cm)
Flower has a dark, conical central disk.

Canada Lily
Lilium canadense
To 5 ft. (1.5 m)

Golden Alexanders
Zizia aurea
To 3 ft. (90 cm)
Small flowers bloom in flat-topped clusters.

Common Mullein
Verbascum thapsus
To 7 ft. (2.1 m)
Common roadside weed.

Common Tansy
Tanacetum vulgare
To 3 ft. (90 cm)
Note fern-like leaves and button-shaped flowers.

PINK & RED FLOWERS

Columbine
Aquilegia canadensis
To 2 ft. (60 cm)

Common Milkweed
Asclepias syriaca
To 6 ft. (1.8 m)
Pink-purple flowers bloom in drooping clusters.

Wild Ginger
Asarum canadense
To 12 in. (30 cm)
Flowers arise at base of 2 leaves.

Spotted Knapweed
Centaurea maculosa
To 4 ft. (1.2 m)
Dark-spotted near flowerhead.

Bull Thistle
Cirsium vulgare
To 6 ft. (1.8 m)

Fireweed
Chamerion angustifolium
To 10 ft. (3 m)
Common in open woodlands and waste areas.

Spring Beauty
Claytonia virginica
To 12 in. (30 cm)

Teasel
Dipsacus spp.
To 7 ft. (2.1 m)

Joe-Pye Weed
Eutrochium maculatum
To 7 ft. (2.1 m)
Flowers are pink to purple. Leaves grow in whorls of 3–5.

Wild Geranium
Geranium maculatum
To 2 ft. (60 cm)

Dame's Rocket
Hesperis matronalis
To 4 ft. (1.2 m)

Small Red Morning Glory
Ipomoea coccinea
Vine to 9 ft. (2.7 m)

PINK & RED FLOWERS

Trumpet Honeysuckle
Lonicera sempervirens
Vine to 17 ft. (5.1 m)

Phlox
Phlox spp.
To 20 in. (50 cm)
Five-petalled, yellow-centered flowers may be white, yellow, pink, red or lavender. Grows in sprawling clusters.

Cardinal Flower
Lobelia cardinalis
To 4 ft. (1.2 m)

Red Trillium
Trillium sessile
To 12 in. (30 cm)
Color varies from red to brown and green. Flower smells like carrion.

Red Clover
Trifolium pratense
To 2 ft. (60 cm)
Leaves have 3 leaflets.

Milkwort
Polygala spp.
To 16 in. (40 cm)

BLUE & PURPLE FLOWERS

Aster
Aster spp.
To 12 in. (30 cm)

Purple Coneflower
Echinacea purpurea
To 5 ft. (1.5 m)

Harebell
Campanula rotundifolia
To 40 in. (1 m)

Spiked Lobelia
Lobelia spicata
To 4 ft. (1.2 m)

Bottle Gentian
Gentiana clausa
To 2 ft. (60 cm)

Wild Hyacinth
Camassia scilloides
To 2 ft. (60 cm)

BLUE & PURPLE FLOWERS

Purple Loosestrife
Lythrum salicaria
To 7 ft. (2.1 m)
Invasive weed is very common in marshes and ponds.

Wild Bergamot
Monarda spp.
To 4 ft. (1.2 m)

Pennywort
Obolaria virginica
To 8 in. (20 cm)
Flowers are white to purplish.

Virginia Bluebells
Mertensia virginica
To 2 ft. (60 cm)

Violet Wood Sorrel
Oxalis violacea
To 6 in. (15 cm)

Pickerelweed
Pontederia cordata
To 4 ft. (1.2 m)
Aquatic plant.

True Forget-me-not
Myosotis scorpioides
To 2 ft. (60 cm)
Small sky-blue flowers have yellow centers.

Spiderwort
Tradescantia spp.
To 3 ft. (90 cm)
Flowers bloom in small clusters at base of leaves.

Ironweed
Vernonia spp.
To 5 ft. (1.5 m)

Blue-eyed Grass
Sisyrinchium angustifolium
To 20 in. (50 cm)

Venus' Looking Glass
Triodanis spp.
To 2 ft. (60 cm)
Note how leaves "clasp" the stem.

Bluets
Houstonia caerulea
To 6 in. (15 cm)

Common Blue Violet
Viola papilionacea
To 8 in. (20 cm)

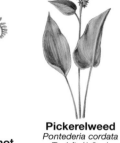

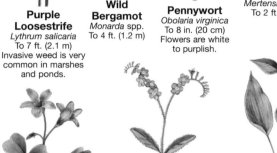

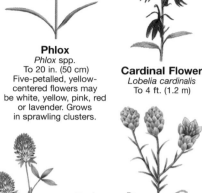